ISBN-13: 978-0-328-50050-5
ISBN-10:   0-328-50050-X
19   20

CONTENTS

To Dan P., who knows how to dress a truck

—J. S.

5

Little Dan Dumper

Little Dan Dumper sat on
   his bumper,
Taking his break for the day.
Along came Pete Loader,
   who revved his loud motor,
And frightened Dan
   Dumper away.

Three **LOUD** Trucks

Three **LOUD** trucks.

Three **LOUD** trucks.

See how they Z O O M.

See how they Z O O M.

They all jumped over the *muck* and *goo*.

They skidded and screeched

and their mufflers blew.

Did you ever see such a crazy crew?

As three **LOUD** trucks.

Three **LOUD** trucks.

GABBY Had a LITTLE BEAR

Gabby had
  a little bear—

Its fur was
  soft and brown.

And everywhere
  that Gabby went,

She took
  her bear to town.

P eter P eter
P ayload Eater

Peter Peter Payload eater
Hit a rock and blew his heater.
He roared into the lake and fell.
And there he cooled off very well.

9

This Is the Way

This is the way we **scoop** the dirt,
scoop the dirt, **scoop** the dirt.
This is the way we **scoop**
the dirt, every
Trucktown
morning.

This is the way we **dump** the dirt,
dump the dirt, **dump** the dirt.
This is the way we **dump** the dirt,
every Trucktown morning.

This is the way we **smooth** the dirt,
smooth the dirt, **smooth** the dirt.
This is the way we **smooth** the dirt,
every Trucktown morning.

This is the way we **zoom** and **play** . .
every Trucktown morning.

10

Patty cake, patty cake, Dumper Dan.
Dump me some dirt as fast as you can.

Slide it and drop it
and mark it DD,

And pile it in the lot for Melvin and me.

SWING Around with ROSIE

Swing around with Rosie.

Swing around with Rosie,

Smashes!

Bashes!

It all falls DOWN!

12

It's Raining, It's Pouring

It's raining, it's pouring.
Monster Max is roaring.

He jumped and slid
And blew his lid
And spun around all morning.

13

JACK AND KAT

Jack and Kat raced up the hill
To burn some crazy rubber.

Jack zoomed down,
Right through Trucktown,
And Kat came scraping after.

Rock~a~Bye Mixer

Rock-a-bye mixer at the site top.

When the wind blows,
   the building will rock.

When the beam breaks,
   the mixer will fall.

And down will come Melvin—
   bricks, beams, and all.

Wrecker Rosie Sat on a Wall

Wrecker Rosie

Wrecker Rosie sat on a wall.
Wrecker Rosie made it all fall.
All the town's tow trucks
And all the town's rigs . . .

Did whatever Rosie said after that.

This Little Truck

This little truck worried about the market.
This little truck worried about home.
This little truck worried about stop signs.
This little truck worried about mud, sharp stones,
    those icky bugs that get squashed in your grill,
    and pretty much everything else in the world.
And this worried truck honked, "Eek! Eek! Eek!"
    all the way home.

Rumble, Rumble, Monster Max

Rumble, rumble, Monster Max.
Can you jump those junkyard stacks?
Up above the trash so high,
Like a rocket in the sky.
Rumble, rumble, Monster Max.
Yep, he jumped those junkyard stacks.

POP! BLOWS THE DIESEL

All around the parking garage,
Pat Pumper chased the Diesel.
Pat Pumper thought it was all
  in truck fun,
Till POP! blows the Diesel.

Pat Pumper with a spool of hose,
And Lucy with her ladder.
That's the way the Truck
  Game goes.
POP! blows the Diesel.

Hickory, Dickory, D🕐ck

Hickory, dickory, dock
Max raced up the block

The clock struck one

The race was done

Hickory, dickory, dock

20

Rub-a-Dub-Dub

Rub-a-dub-dub,
    three trucks in a tub.

And who do you think they'd be?

The Pumper, the Ladder,
    and little sis, Rita.
The Fire and Rescue trucks three.

21

FIRE TRUCKS
ARE
RED

Fire trucks are red.

Max Truck is blue.

Gabby is pink.

(How about you?)

22

Hey Diddle Diddle

Hey diddle diddle, the truck in the middle
Thought ice cream made up the moon.
The little truck laughed
To see such a sight
And sang his You-Know-What tune.

That's What **Trucks** Are Made of

M etal and stuff and everything tough—
That's what trucks are made of.

Play by the **ton**, and everything **fun**—
That's what trucks are made of.